Adrienne Barman

CREATUREPEDIA

WELCOME TO THE GREATEST SHOW ON EARTH

WIDE EYED EDITIONS

Contents

CREATUREPEDIA celebrates the amazing array of animals that grace our planet. Sadly, some are now under threat, some are already extinct (and one or two may never have existed in the first place!) but each one has its own unique part to play in the animal kingdom...

Turn the page to see the greatest show on Earth and discover who is the biggest, the brainiest, and the most beautiful of them all.

The architects

Social weaver
builds the largest nest of any bird

The architects

Beaver
builds a dam from logs, mud and stones to keep predators away

Weaver ant
works with others to weave leaves together to make a nest

Prairie dog burrow has sleeping chambers, nursery chambers and chambers for hiding from hunters

Taveta weaver male weaver builds nest; female chooses mate based on quality of nest

Spider spins a strong web

Mason wasp female builds a tiny mud nest, stocked with food, for each of her eggs

The architects

Red ovenbird builds a mud nest that looks like a wood-fired oven

Sand martin burrows a nest in a sandy cliff face

Termite works with others to build enormous mounds

The big-eared beasts

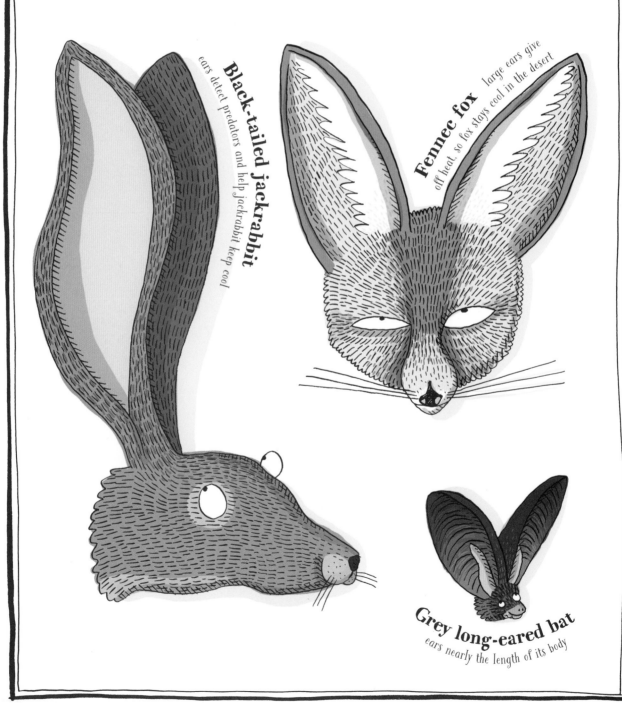

Black-tailed jackrabbit
ears detect predators and help jackrabbit keep cool

Fennec fox large ears give off heat, so fox stays cool in the desert

Grey long-eared bat
ears nearly the length of its body

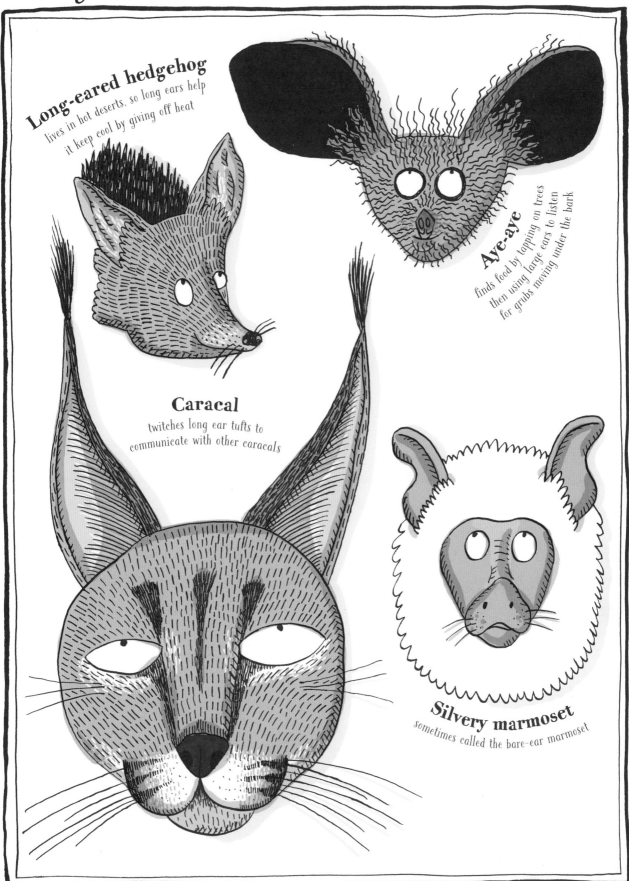

Long-eared hedgehog
lives in hot deserts, so long ears help
it keep cool by giving off heat

Aye-aye
finds food by tapping on trees
then using large ears to listen
for grubs moving under the bark

Caracal
twitches long ear tufts to
communicate with other caracals

Silvery marmoset
sometimes called the bare-ear marmoset

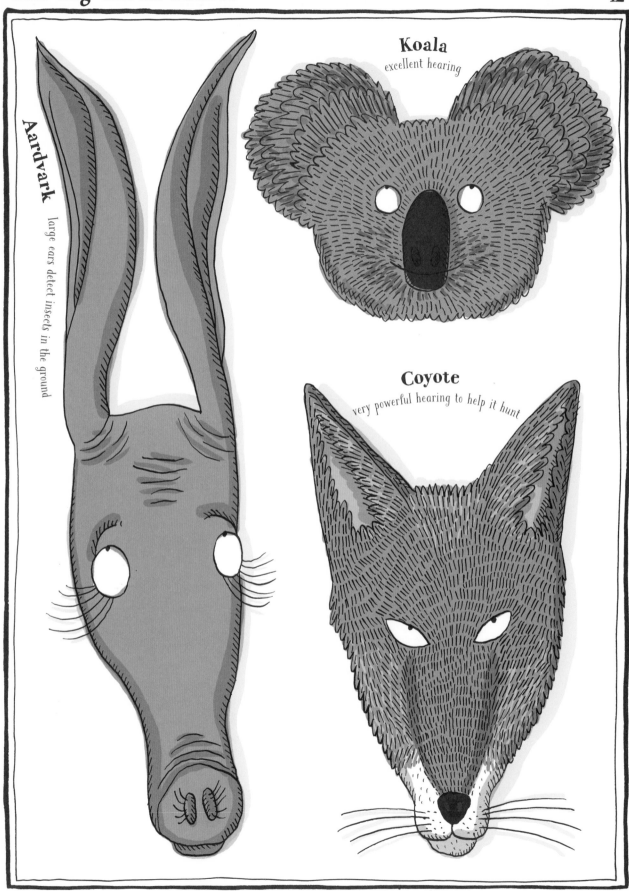

Koala
excellent hearing

Aardvark
large ears detect insects in the ground

Coyote
very powerful hearing to help it hunt

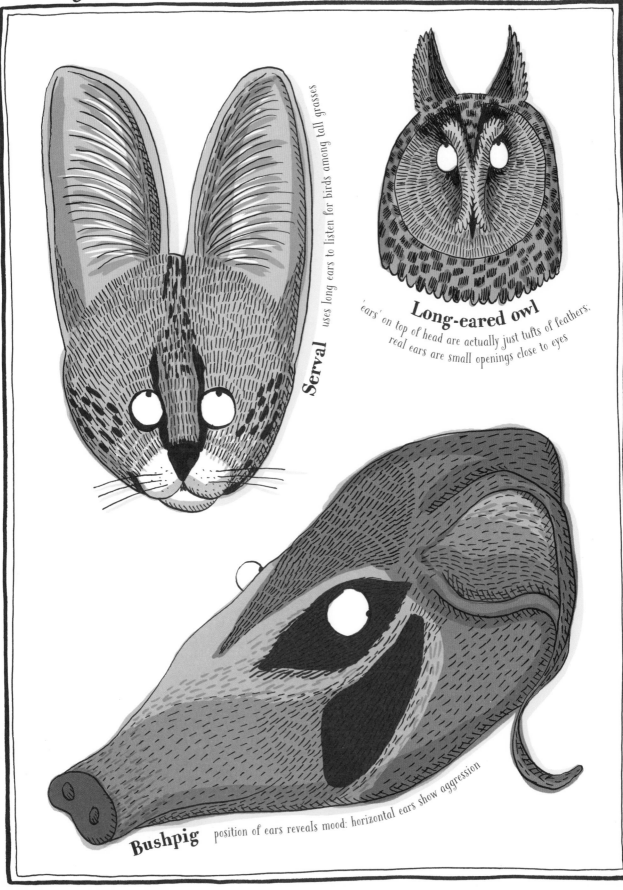

Serval uses long ears to listen for birds among tall grasses

Long-eared owl 'ears' on top of head are actually just tufts of feathers; real ears are small openings close to eyes

Bushpig position of ears reveals mood: horizontal ears show aggression

Helmeted guineafowl

Natterjack toad

male call can be heard
several kilometres away

Field cricket
makes sounds by rubbing
its wings together

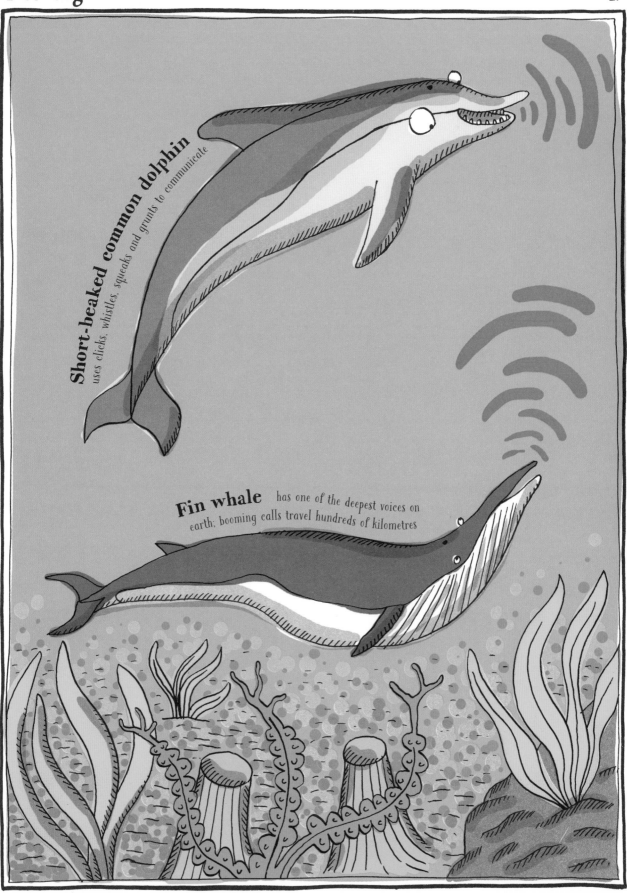

Short-beaked common dolphin uses clicks, whistles, squeaks and grunts to communicate

Fin whale has one of the deepest voices on earth: booming calls travel hundreds of kilometres

Cory's shearwater

Scarlet macaw

Bumblebee

Howler monkey

Cicada
one of the noisiest insects in the world; can make a sound over 100 decibels!

Rattlesnake
has hollow segments on the end of its tail that knock together to make rattling sound

White-fronted goose

The blue beauties

Victoria crowned pigeon

Broad-bodied darter dragonfly (male)

Blue shark

Blue sea star

The blue beauties

Azure damselfly

Common blue butterfly

Blue morpho butterfly

African blue flycatcher (male)

Blue poison-dart frog

Turquoise honeycreeper (male)

Bluebottle

Rainbow agama (male)

Woodland kingfisher

Blue surgeonfish

Blue tit

Puma
can leap up to 6 m / 20 ft
from a standing start

Kangaroo
the only large animal that uses jumping
as main means of getting around

Flying frog
glides between trees using large
webbed feet as parachutes

Atlantic salmon
leaps upstream to get to
breeding grounds

Springbok
can leap up to 4 m / 13 ft into the air

Merriam's kangaroo rat
uses large hind feet to leap
more than 1.8 m / 6 ft

Ibex
sure-footed mountain goat,
can jump across crevices

Hare
jumps long distances, can
run at up to 70 kmph / 43 mph

Jerboa
can jump up to 3 m / 10 ft

The brainboxes

The canary-yellows

American yellow warbler

Kinkajou

Golden oriole (male)

Pumpkin toadlet

Pineapple fish

The champion breath-holders

Walrus *30 minutes*

The champion breath-holders

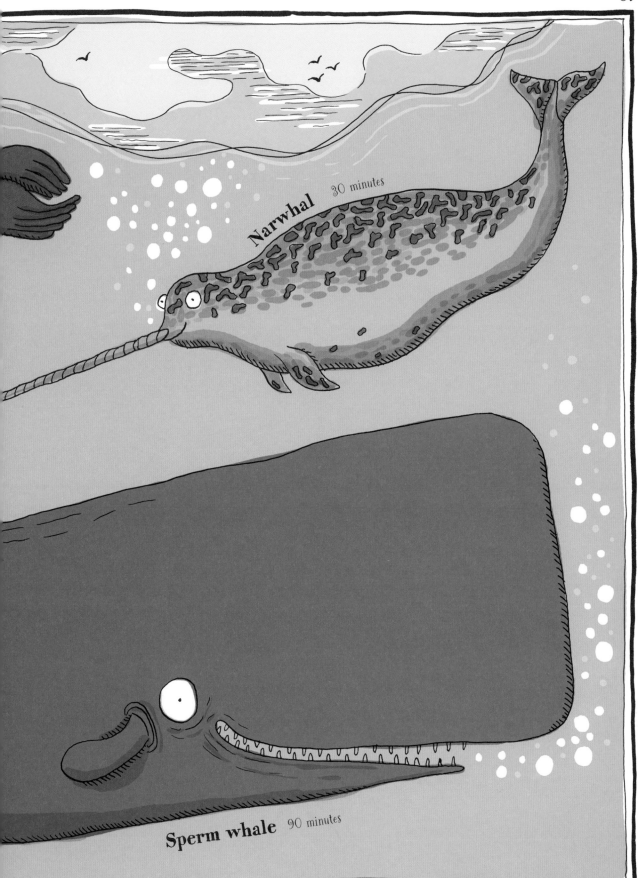

Narwhal 30 minutes

Sperm whale 90 minutes

Hippopotamus
5 minutes

Alligator snapping turtle
40-50 minutes

American alligator
60 minutes

The coal-blacks

Carrion crow

Black bear

Capricorn beetle

Violet ground beetle

The coal-blacks

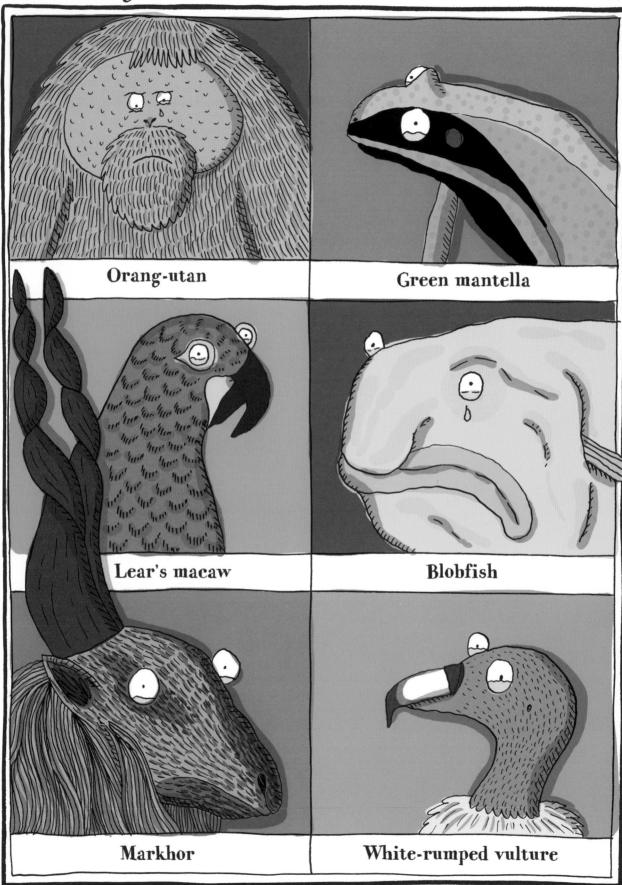

Orang-utan

Green mantella

Lear's macaw

Blobfish

Markhor

White-rumped vulture

Southern cassowary

Saw-tailed bush cricket

Hawaiian monk seal

Drill

Basking shark

Chuckwalla

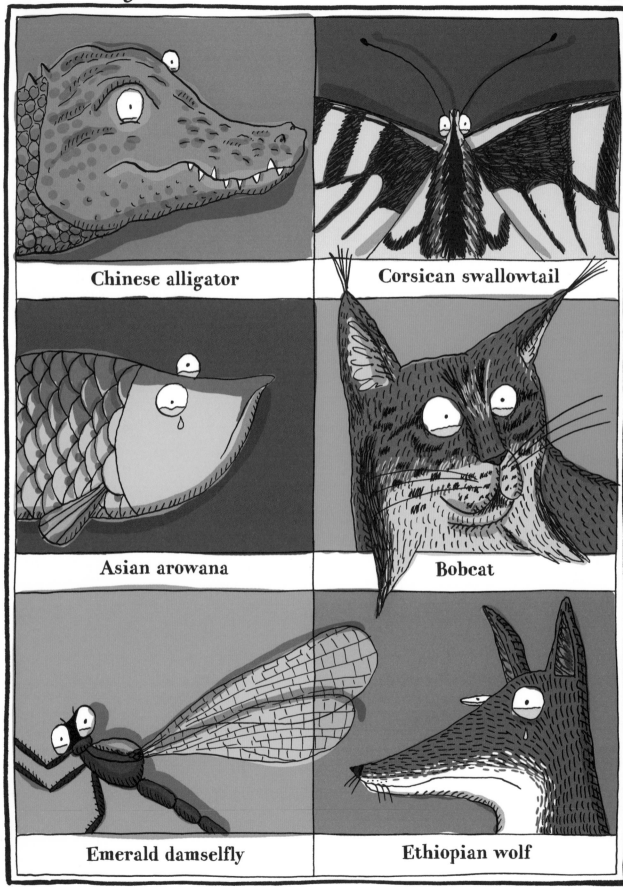

Chinese alligator

Corsican swallowtail

Asian arowana

Bobcat

Emerald damselfly

Ethiopian wolf

The endangered

Snow leopard

Golden lion tamarin

Monkey-eating eagle

Hermit beetle

Green sea turtle

Otter

European green lizard

Kakapo

Rose chafer beetle

The emerald-greens

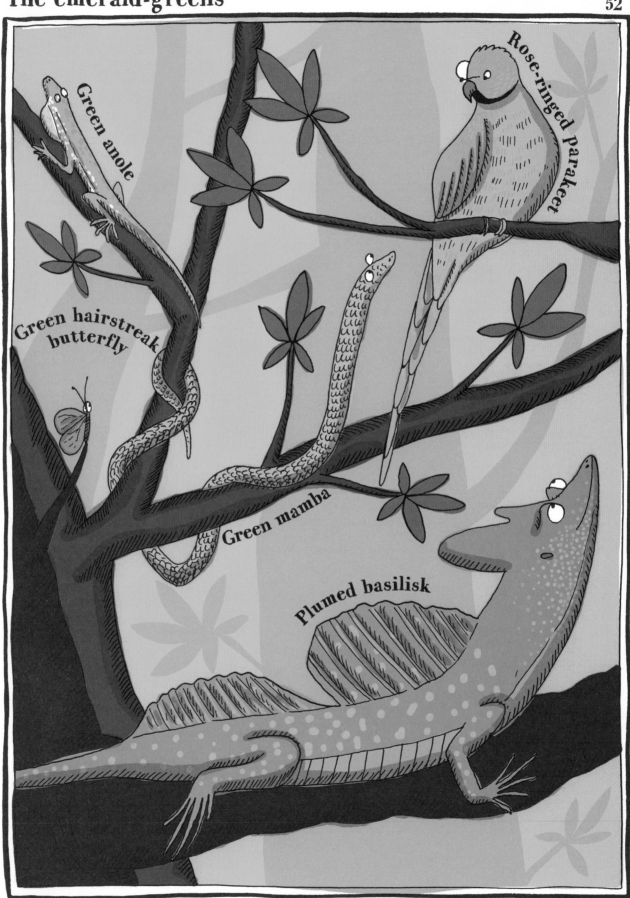

Emerald toucanet

Greenbottle

Green tiger beetle

Emerald tree boa

Green shield bug

Green broadbill

The faithful

Agile gibbon
pairs stay together for life and make a family group with their young

Lovebird
mates for life; often preens and feeds its partner

Dik-dik pairs mate for life and are rarely seen apart

Mongolian gerbil

Wandering albatross

Whooper swan

Mandarin duck

Sea horse

Common crane
pairs make bonds that may last whole lives

Corsac fox
mates help care for the young

Patagonian mara

The faithful

Harpy eagle
mates for life; parents raise only one chick every two to three years

Eastern woolly lemur

Mimic poison frog
both parents care for tadpoles for several months

Common raccoon
female takes only one mate per year

Our family friends

Sheep

Cormorant *used for fishing in China*

Donkey

European rabbit

Chinchilla

Green iguana

Guinea pig

Domestic cat

Dog

Goat

Llama
used for transport and wool

Cow

Water buffalo
used to plough fields, and for milk

Horse

Camel

The fierce

Sparrowhawk

Horsefly

Leech

Olive baboon

Asian hornet

Mosquito

Tasmanian devil

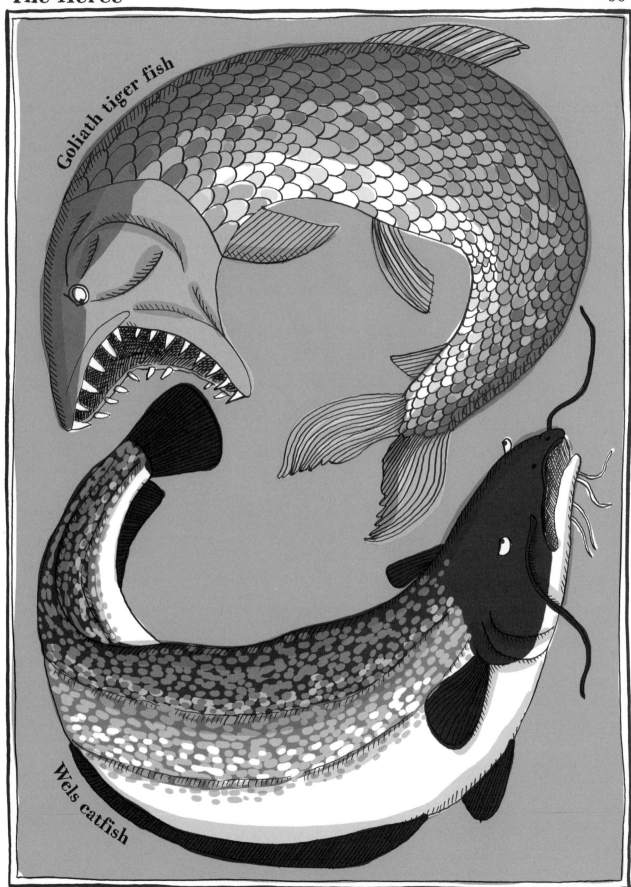

Goliath tiger fish

Wels catfish

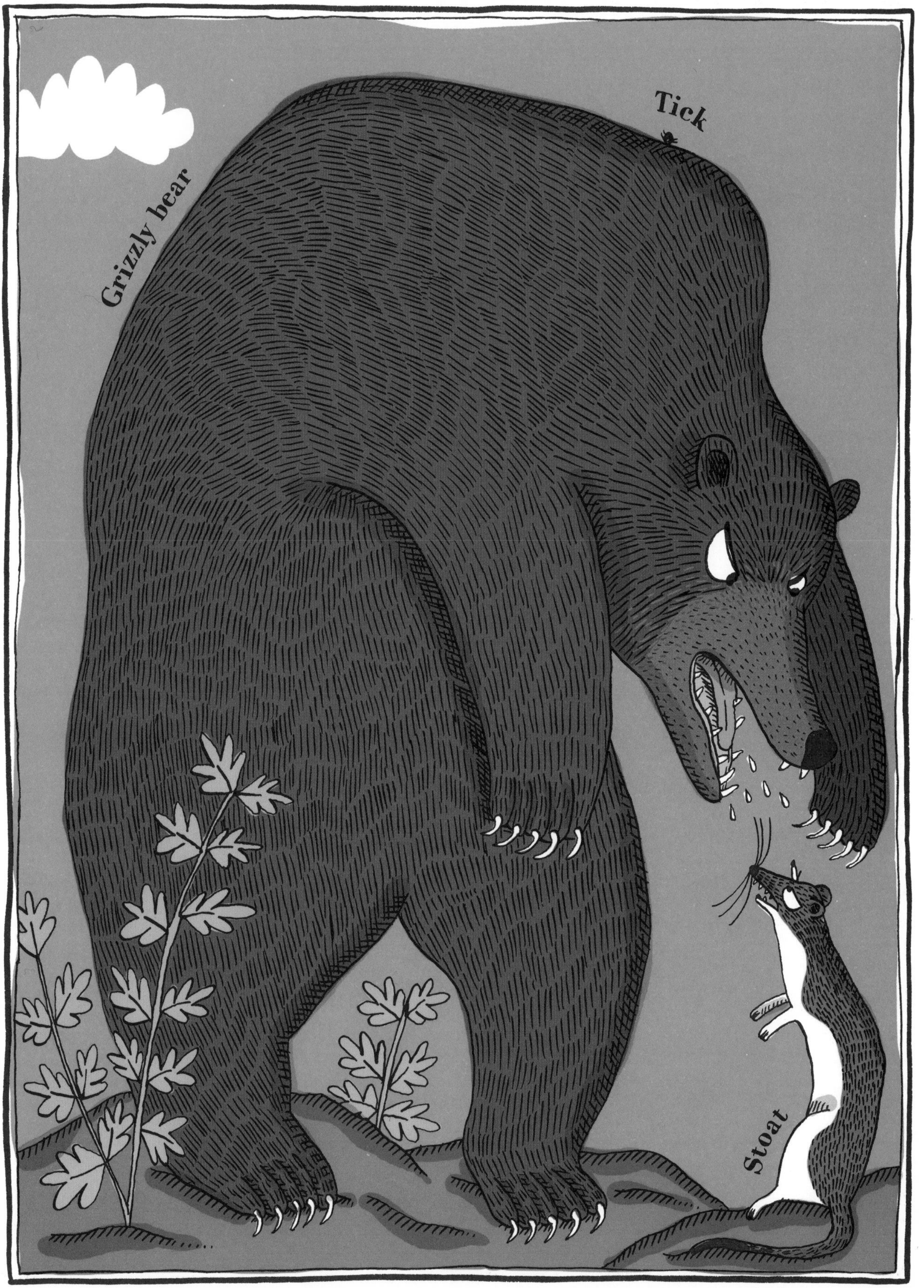
Tick
Grizzly bear
Stoat

Kestrel

Inland taipan

The fierce

The foresters

Roe deer

European rhinoceros beetle

Spring peeper

Indri

Loris

Grove snail

Red squirrel

Emerald tree monitor

Edible doormouse

Valerio's glass frog

Sable

Stag beetle

Malayan tapir

Eurasian woodcock

Bohemian waxwing

Turtle dove

Rosalia longicorn

Wild turkey

Common wombat

The giants

Giant Pacific octopus

world's largest octopus: up to 9 m / 30 ft across

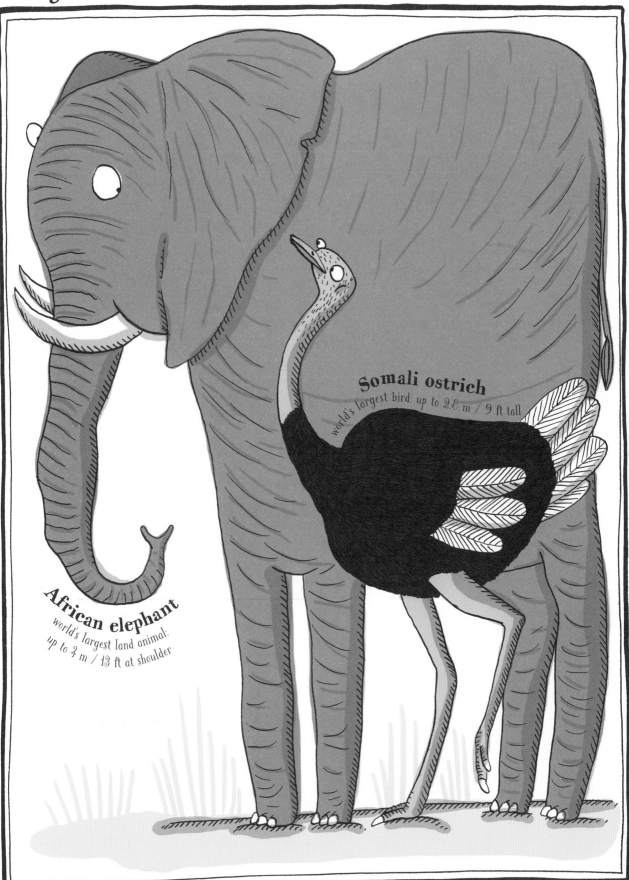

Somali ostrich
world's largest bird: up to 2.8 m / 9 ft tall

African elephant
world's largest land animal:
up to 4 m / 13 ft at shoulder

Goliath bird-eating spider
up to 28 cm / 11 in legspan

Goliath frog
world's largest frog: up to 33 cm / 13 in long

Chinese giant salamander
world's largest amphibian: up to 1.8 m / 6 ft long

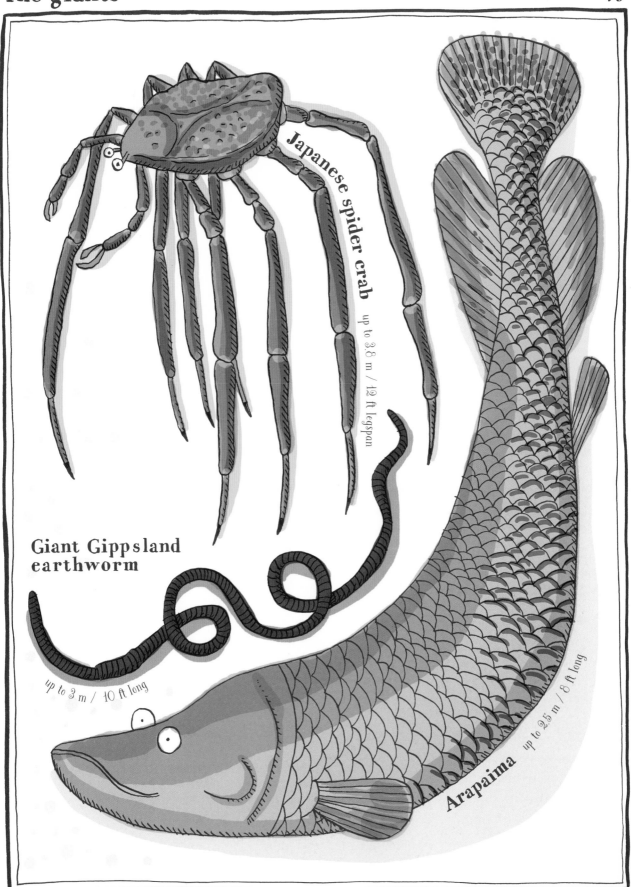

Japanese spider crab up to 3.8 m / 12 ft legspan

Giant Gippsland earthworm

up to 3 m / 10 ft long

Arapaima up to 2.5 m / 8 ft long

The giants

Blue whale
largest animal ever to have lived: up to 33 m / 108 ft long

Whale shark
world's largest fish: up to 12 m / 40 ft long

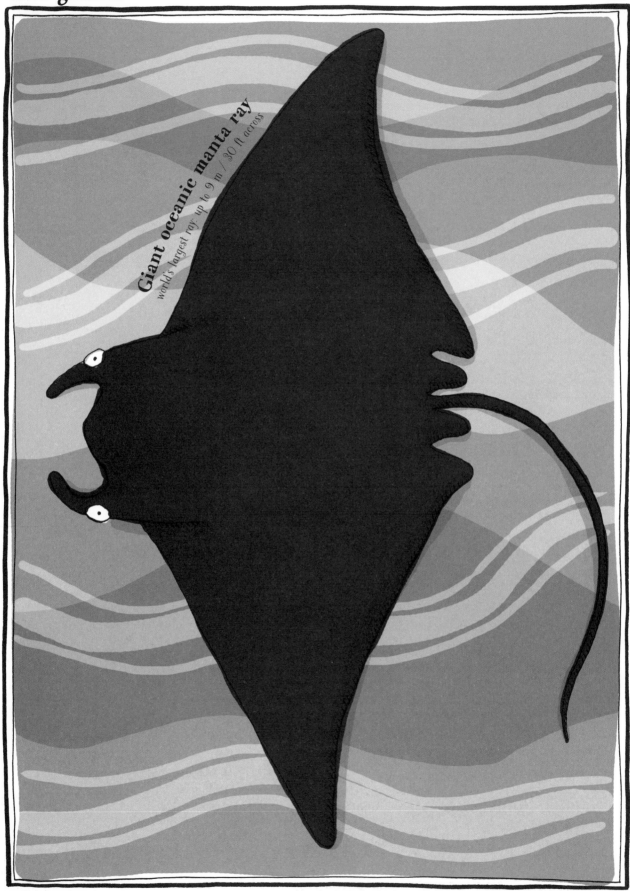

Giant oceanic manta ray

world's largest ray: up to 9 m / 30 ft across

Titan beetle
up to 16.7 cm / 6.5 in long

Capybara
world's largest rodent: up to 1.3 m / 4 ft long

Gorilla
world's largest primate: up to 1.8 m / 6 ft tall

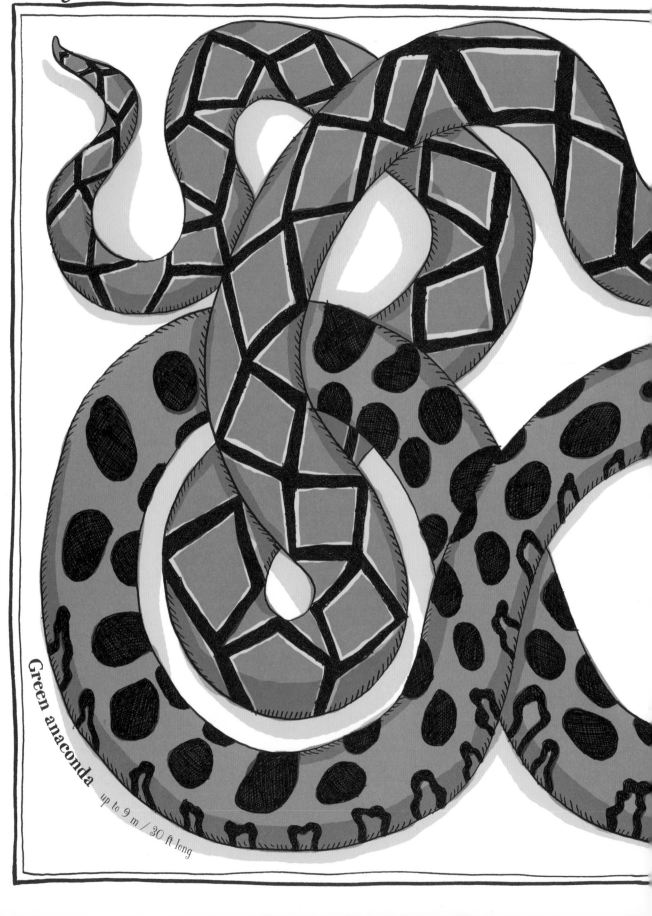

Green anaconda up to 9 m / 30 ft long

Reticulated python up to 10 m / 33 ft long

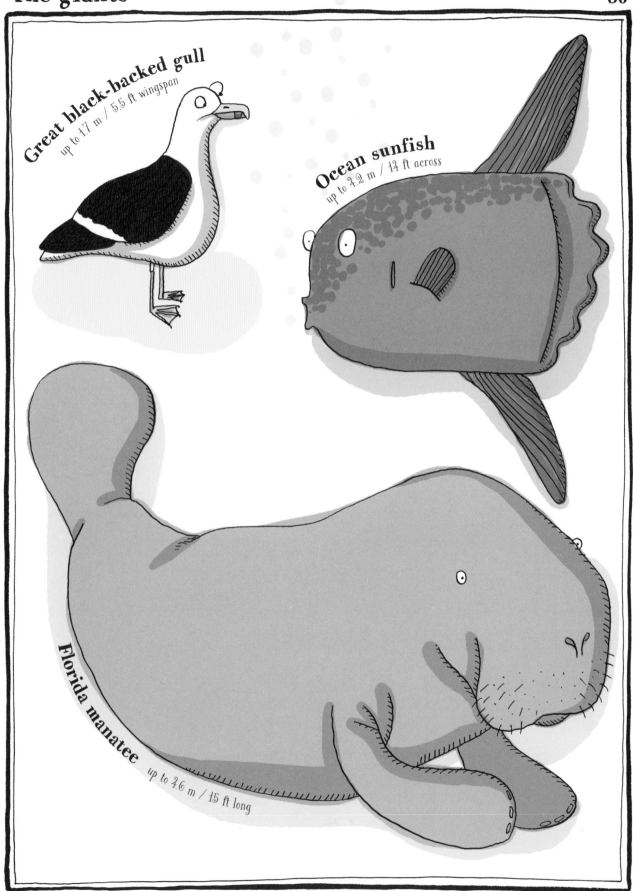

Great black-backed gull
up to 1.7 m / 5.5 ft wingspan

Ocean sunfish
up to 4.2 m / 14 ft across

Florida manatee up to 4.6 m / 15 ft long

The gladiators

Musk ox herd forms a tight circle, facing outwards, for defence; bulls will sometimes charge at attackers

Frilled dragon
if frightened, opens mouth wide
and spreads out neck frill to
scare off attackers

Rubber boa
confuses attackers by pretending
its tail is its head

**Nine-banded
armadillo**
curls into an armoured ball to
protect itself

Cuban tree frog
oozes a toxic slime

Spanish fly
*oozes a blistering poison
from its leg joints*

Ring-necked snake
plays dead when threatened

Striped skunk
squirts a foul-smelling liquid as a defence

Giant pangolin *rolls itself into a ball for defence*

Oriental fire-bellied toad *when threatened, lies on its back to reveal its red belly, which warns predators of its toxic slime*

Woodlouse *curls into a ball when frightened*

Opossum *plays dead to protect itself*

The gladiators

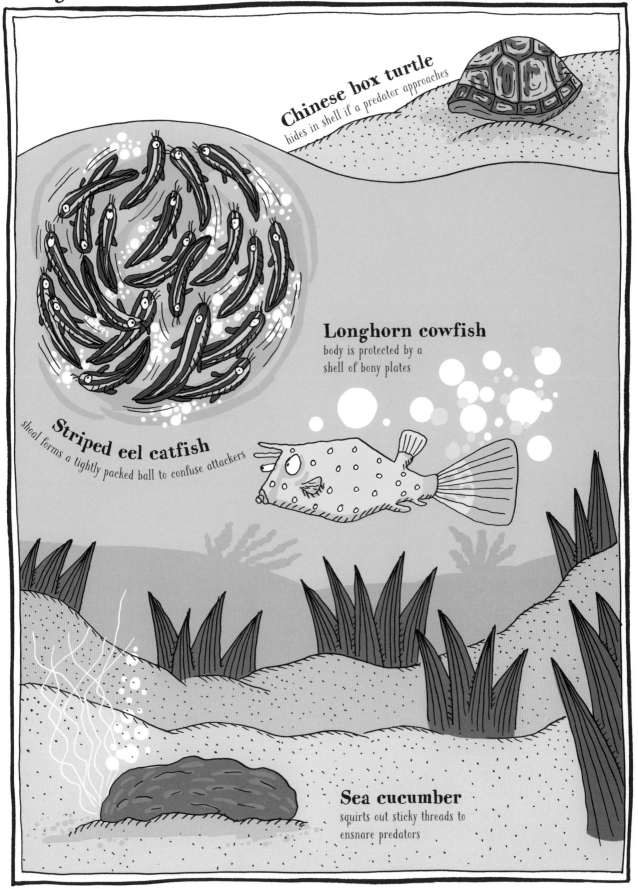

Chinese box turtle
hides in shell if a predator approaches

Longhorn cowfish
body is protected by a
shell of bony plates

Striped eel catfish
shoal forms a tightly packed ball to confuse attackers

Sea cucumber
squirts out sticky threads to
ensnare predators

The homebodies

Wild boar
remains in one territory, leaving only if food runs short

Dugong
good memory allows it to return to same place after long travels

Sea sponge
young sponges drift in the water, adults are attached to seabed

Crayfish
vigorously defends burrow from intruders

Red scorpionfish
does not stray far from its territory

Oyster
lives with others on seabed, forming an oyster reef

Moray eel
aggressive if burrow is disturbed

Magpie
breeding pairs have territory of about 5 hectares / 12 acres

Hermann's tortoise
strong homing instinct

Common kingfisher
very territorial: controls a stretch of river

The Lilliputians

Etruscan shrew
world's smallest mammal: 4 cm / 1.6 in
long (not including tail)

Red panda
56 cm / 22 in long
(not including tail)

Lesser white-fronted goose
60 cm / 24 in long

Little penguin
33 cm / 13 in tall

Spined pygmy shark 20 cm / 8 in

Candiru 5 cm / 2 in long

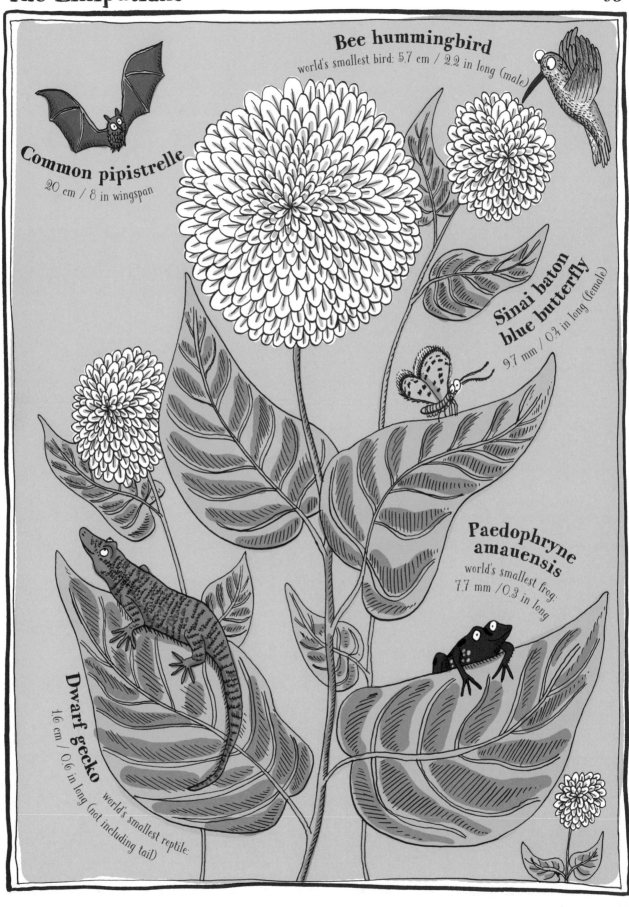

Bee hummingbird
world's smallest bird: 5.7 cm / 2.2 in long (male)

Common pipistrelle
20 cm / 8 in wingspan

Sinai baton blue butterfly
9.7 mm / 0.3 in long (female)

Paedophryne amauensis
world's smallest frog:
7.7 mm / 0.3 in long

Dwarf gecko
16 cm / 0.6 in long
world's smallest reptile
(not including tail)

Pygmy falcon
19 cm / 7.5 in long

Galapagos sea lion
2 m / 6.5 ft long

Pygmy hippopotamus
80 cm / 31 in at shoulder

Pony
less than 127 cm / 58 in at shoulder

Alpaca
90 cm / 35 in at shoulder

The long-necked

Dromedary camel
long neck helps it reach high branches to feed

Waller's gazelle
can reach high branches
for leaves

Californian sea lion
long, flexible neck makes it an agile swimmer

Purple heron
extends long neck to
catch fish

Mute swan can't dive, so uses neck to reach food on lake and riverbeds

Great egret tucks neck in when flying

Great crested grebe neck helps reach fish when diving under water

Eastern long-necked turtle neck allows it to breathe at surface while body is hidden under water

Guanaco
skin on neck is extra-thick to protect against puma bites

Greater rhea
can easily scan for danger thanks to long neck

Giraffe weevil (male)
uses neck for fighting other males and building a nest

The long-tongued

Black woodpecker
tongue = 10 cm / 4 in

Okapi tongue = 35 cm / 14 in

Ruby-throated hummingbird *extendible tongue*

Giant anteater tongue = 60 cm / 24 in

Giraffe tongue = 50 cm / 20 in

Chameleon tongue is longer than body

Sun bear tongue = 25 cm / 10 in

Honey possum brush-tipped tongue collects pollen

The masters of camouflage

Bush cricket

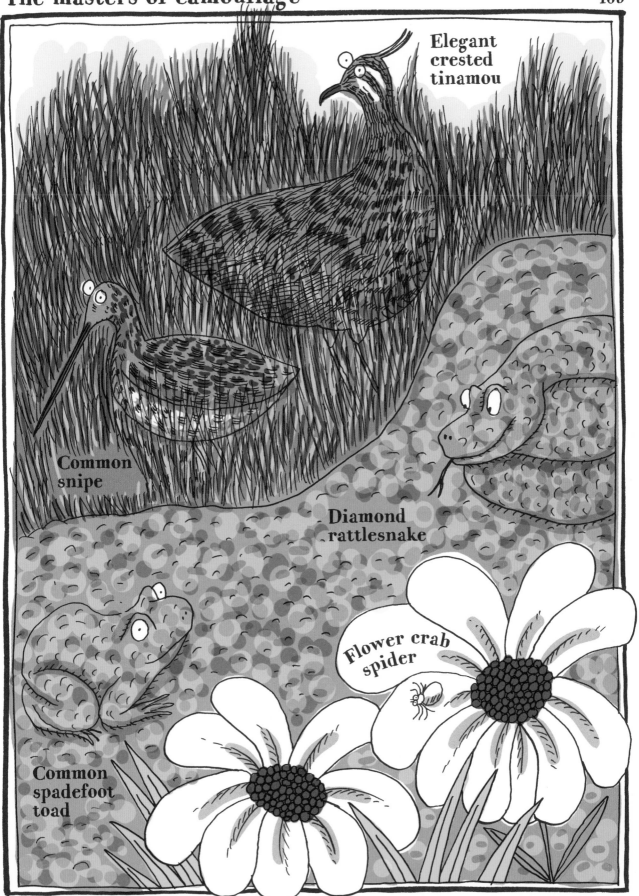

Jaguar

The mountaineers

Yak
thick hair keeps it warm in snowy mountains

Cape mountain zebra
world's smallest zebra; lives in mountains of South Africa

Apollo butterfly
lives in flowery meadows among mountain ranges

Black-chested buzzard eagle
uses strong air currents to soar among mountain peaks

Andean condor
huge 3-m (10-ft) wingspan; glides on air currents

Rock ptarmigan
moults to change colour so blends in as seasons turn

Marmot
hibernates in group burrow during freezing winter

The munch-it-uppers

Tiger hunts in darkness with night vision six times better than humans'

Barracuda *dagger-like teeth*

Orca *tips up ice floes to knock seals and penguins into water to eat*

Swordfish *uses swordlike bill to slash at prey*

Leopard seal uses sharp teeth to grip penguins, shaking them vigorously to kill them

Starfish prises open shellfish using five arms

Little owl may attack prey larger than itself

Chinese water dragon sticky tongue helps it catch and hold prey

Black-footed ferret stealthy, burrow-raiding hunter of prairie dogs

Red fox
silently stalks a victim then pounces suddenly

Bald eagle
swoops down and scoops fish from water using sharp talons

Saltwater crocodile
largest reptile in the world, fearsome predator

Montagu's harrier
drops from sky to catch prey by surprise

Muskellunge
eats prey head first, sometimes in a single massive gulp

Dragon

Snouter
small mammal that uses nose
for everything including jumping
and fishing

The mythical

Griffin

Lernaean Hydra

Baku
eater of nightmares

The night owls

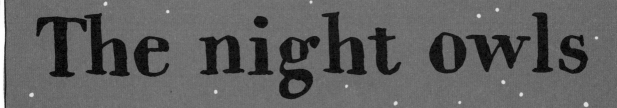

Eurasian eagle-owl
night vision, powerful hearing and silent
flight make it a deadly predator

The night owls

Philippine tarsier
head can swivel nearly all the way round to look about

Hazel dormouse
large eyes and ears help it survive in dark

Millipede
most have between 80 and 300 legs

Coral snake
one of world's most venomous snakes

Giant peacock moth
largest moth in Europe

Sloth

world's slowest mamaml: spends most of life hanging upside down

Badger
strong sense of smell helps
it find food in dark

Crocodile gecko

European conger eel

Asian tree toad
toes have sticky discs that
help it climb trees

Red-eyed tree frog
sleeps during day with red
eyes closed, to hide from hunters

Brazilian tapir
hides in water to avoid attackers, using snout as a snorkel

Stone loach

Squirrelfish

Kiwi
shy, flightless bird, lives only in New Zealand

Spanish moon moth

Barn owl

excellent hearing helps it find prey even in pitch dark; one ear is slightly higher than other, helping owl pinpoint sounds

The pack animals

Grey langur
troops can be mixed or
all-male

Puffin
breeds in large colonies of up to a million nests

Jackal
lives as part of a pair but
often hunts in a pack

Atlantic cod
female lays up to 9 million eggs each spawning season

The pack animals

Przewalski's horse
wild horse; family groups form
herds that travel together

Ring-tailed lemur
groups can contain up to
30 lemurs

Clown loach
lives in large shoals in Indonesian waters

Hippopotamus
groups, called pods, can contain 100 hippos

European honeybee
lives in a hive of up to 80,000

Addax
lives in a herd of up to 20

Bearded dragon
gathers in groups to feed or sunbathe

Processionary caterpillar
up to 300 caterpillars can march in single file, nose to tail

American bison
herds can number thousands

Oriental cockroach
gathers to rest in groups during the day

Herring
swims in a huge shoal of up to 4 billion!

Meerkat
lives in groups of up to 50 in large burrows

Midwife toad
male carries eggs on back till they are ready to hatch

Mandrill
groups, called hordes, often contain hundreds of monkeys

The pack animals

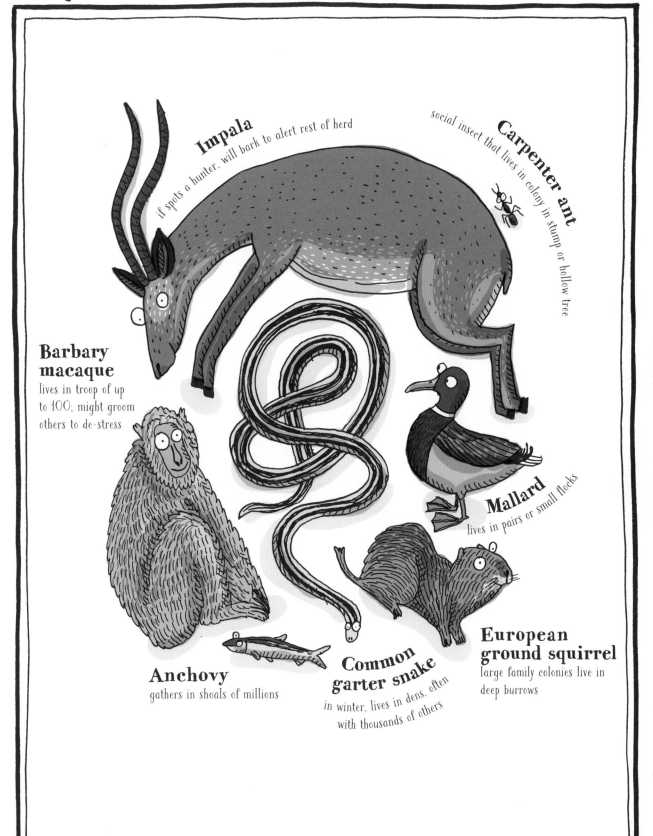

Impala
if spots a hunter, will bark to alert rest of herd

Carpenter ant
social insect that lives in colony in stump or hollow tree

Barbary macaque
lives in troop of up to 100; might groom others to de-stress

Mallard
lives in pairs or small flocks

Anchovy
gathers in shoals of millions

Common garter snake
in winter, lives in dens, often with thousands of others

European ground squirrel
large family colonies live in deep burrows

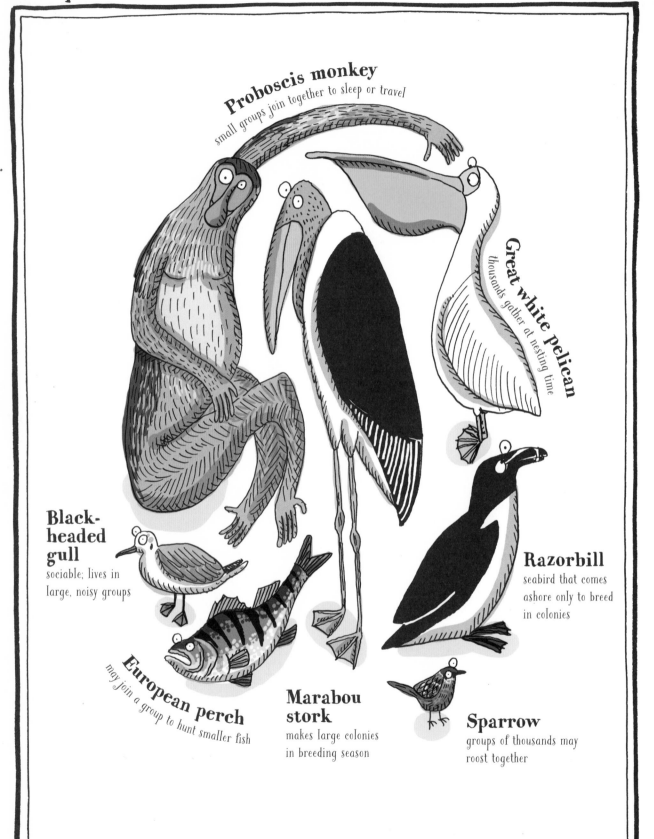

Proboscis monkey
small groups join together to sleep or travel

Great white pelican
thousands gather at nesting time

Black-headed gull
sociable; lives in large, noisy groups

Razorbill
seabird that comes ashore only to breed in colonies

European perch
may join a group to hunt smaller fish

Marabou stork
makes large colonies in breeding season

Sparrow
groups of thousands may roost together

Cuban solenodon
venomous saliva

Six-spot burnet moth
contains cyanide

Scorpion
venomous sting

Hooded pitohui
toxic skin and feathers

Blue-spotted ribbontail ray
venomous tail spines

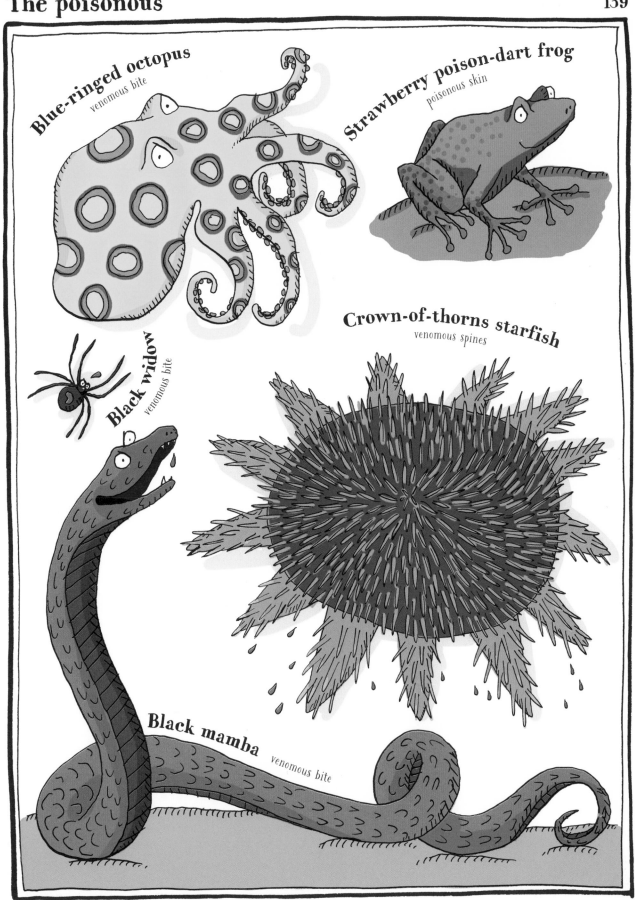

Blue-ringed octopus
venomous bite

Strawberry poison-dart frog
poisonous skin

Crown-of-thorns starfish
venomous spines

Black widow
venomous bite

Black mamba *venomous bite*

The poisonous

The poisonous

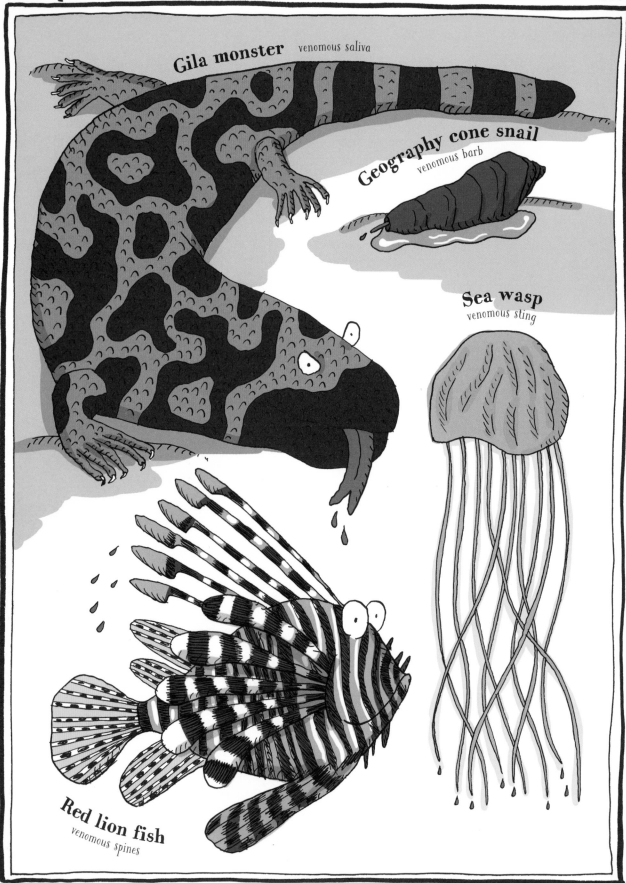

Gila monster *venomous saliva*

Geography cone snail *venomous barb*

Sea wasp *venomous sting*

Red lion fish *venomous spines*

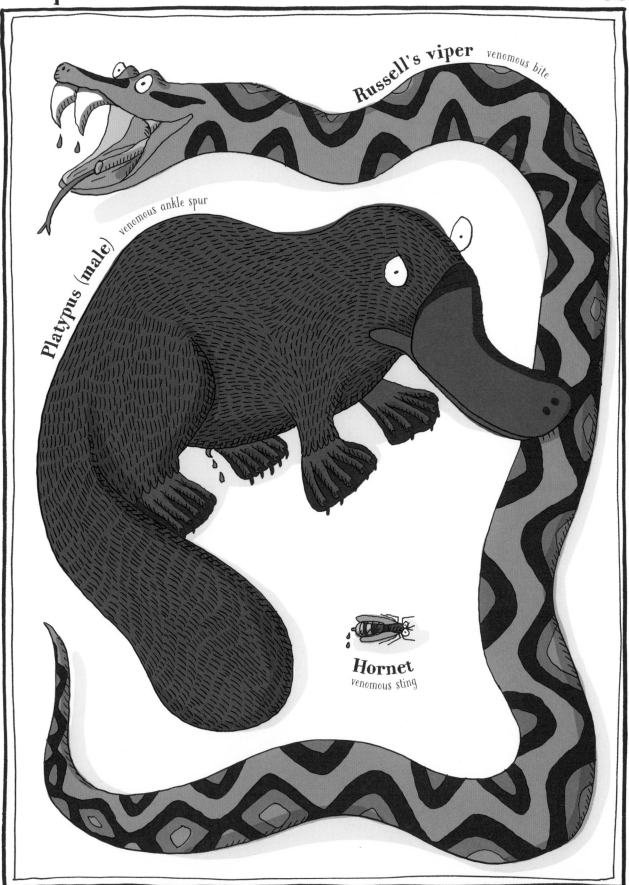

Russell's viper *venomous bite*

Platypus (**male**) *venomous ankle spur*

Hornet
venomous sting

The pretty-in-pinks

Pig

The prickly ones

Spiny anteater
spiky body; some even have spines on tongue to snare prey

European hedgehog
if afraid, will curl into a ball with 6,000 spines sticking out

Armadillo lizard
can put tail in mouth and roll into a prickly ball

Bay shrimp
has a spiky horn above eyes

Crested porcupine
has tiny barbs on end of quills
that stick into flesh, making
them hard to remove

The prickly ones

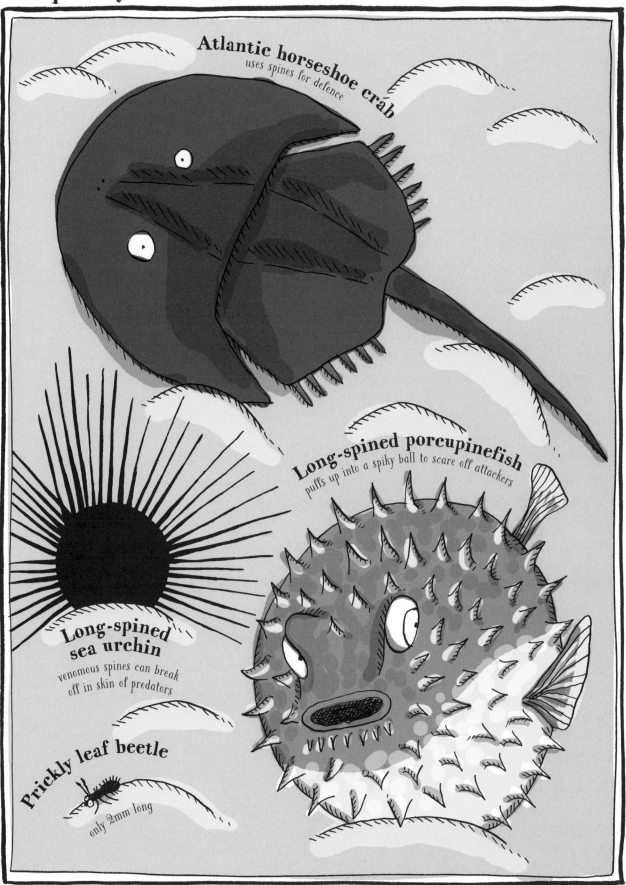

Atlantic horseshoe crab
uses spines for defence

Long-spined porcupinefish
puffs up into a spiky ball to scare off attackers

Long-spined sea urchin
venomous spines can break off in skin of predators

Prickly leaf beetle
only 2mm long

Horned desert viper horns fold back to give snake smoother shape for burrowing

Horned lizard puffs up and sticks out spikes to scare off attackers; can also squirt blood from eyes!

The redheads

Milk snake

Cardinal beetle

Northern cardinal (male)

Crimson rosella

Scarlet tanager

Vermilion flycatcher

Poplar leaf beetle

Tomato frog

Orange roughy

Red weevil

Scarlet ibis

Firebug

Red salamander

The regal

Lion

Emperor scorpion

Golden eagle

Emperor angelfish

King snake

White tiger

Emperor penguin

Crowned sandgrouse

King cobra

Royal python

The show-offs

Western parotia
spreads out feathers like a tutu and does a
ballet-like dance to attract females

Red-capped manakin
moonwalks along a branch
to impress

Common pheasant
male circles female with tail
fanned out

Satin bowerbird
male builds bower decorated
with bright objects to
attract a mate

Marten
male chases female
through the trees

Red deer

stag bellows to warn off other males and attract females

Wood grouse
makes clicking, popping, scraping
sounds as part of mating ritual

Superb lyrebird
male fans tail, dances and sings
to impress a mate

Magnificent frigate bird
male puffs up red throat-pouch like a balloon

Peacock
female chooses mate with largest, most impressive tail fan

Common toad
male puffs up throat to make mating call

Stickleback
male does a zigzag courtship dance

Toco toucan
male offers female gifts of food

Grey-crowned crane
bows, jumps and dances

The snowy-whites

Polar bear

White cockatoo

Swan moth

Greenhouse
whitefly

Cabbage white butterfly

Ivory gull

Rocky Mountain goat

Arctic fox (winter coat)

Snowy owl

Snowy sheathbill

Snowshoe hare (winter coat)

Moon jellyfish

Beluga whale

The solitary

Nile monitor

Black vulture

Brown bear

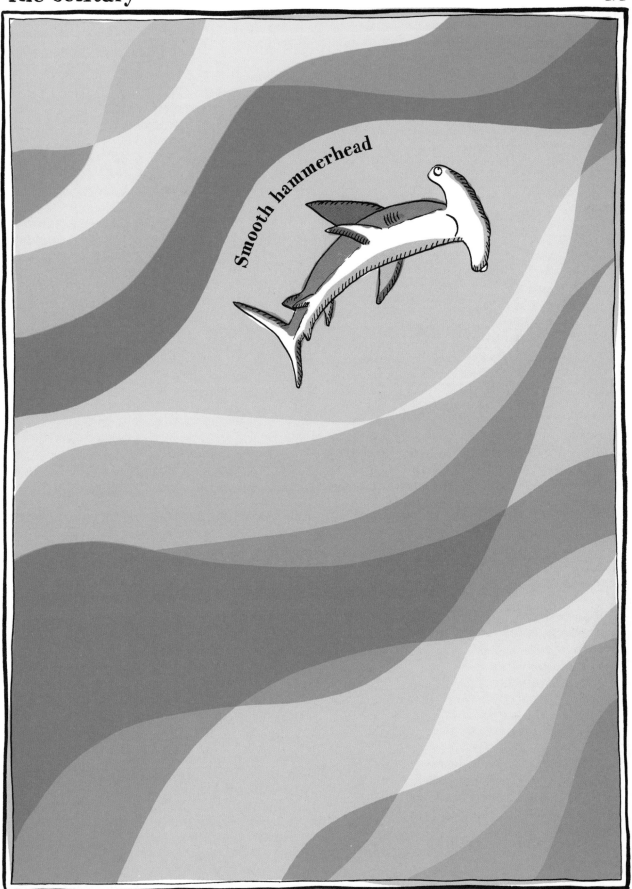

Giant grouper

Praying mantis

The solitary

Mole

Common shrew

Boa constrictor

Leopard

Digger wasp

Galapagos giant tortoise

Lobster

The spotted

Peacock-eye stingray

Spotted scat

Humpback grouper

Fallow deer

Tiger salamander

Silver-washed
fritillary butterfly

Marsh fly

Quoll

Leopard slug

Leopard gecko

The sprinters

Common swift
up to 111.6kmph / 69.3 mph

Cheetah
up to 102 kmph / 64 mph

Warthog
up to 48 kmph / 30 mph

Peregrine falcon
up to 389 kmph / 242 mph

Moose
up to
56 kmph / 35 mph

Common noctule
up to 50 kmph / 31 mph

Saiga antelope
up to 80 kmph / 50 mph

Quail
up to 80 kmph / 50 mph

Dragonfly
up to 97 kmph / 60 mph

Red Sea ghost crab
up to 16 kmph / 10 mph

Mako shark
up to 74 kmph / 46 mph

Tuna
up to 75 kmph /
47 mph

Common ostrich
up to 70 kmph /
43 mph

Rhinoceros
up to 48 kmph / 30 mph

Greater roadrunner
up to 42 kmph / 26 mph

The stripy

Grevy's zebra

Aardwolf

Striped hyena

Moorish idol

Copperband
butterfly fish

Sheepshead

Fiji banded iguana

Bandy-bandy

Banded sea krait

Leopard ground squirrel

Barred antshrike

Numbat

Banded mongoose

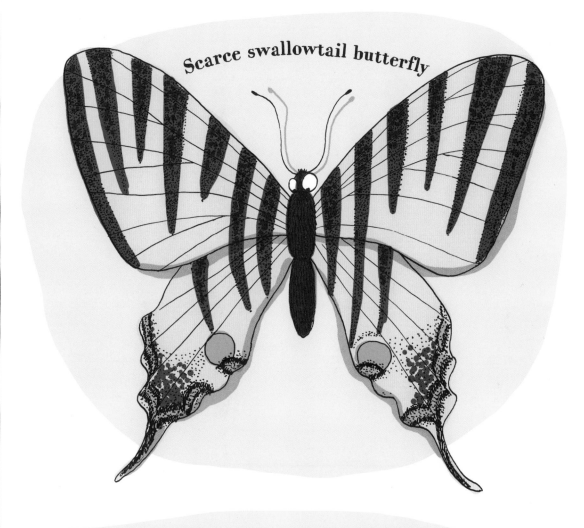

Scarce swallowtail butterfly

Chequered beetle

Striped cucumber beetle

Minstrel bug

Colorado potato beetle

The unlucky

Rock dove
believed to carry diseases

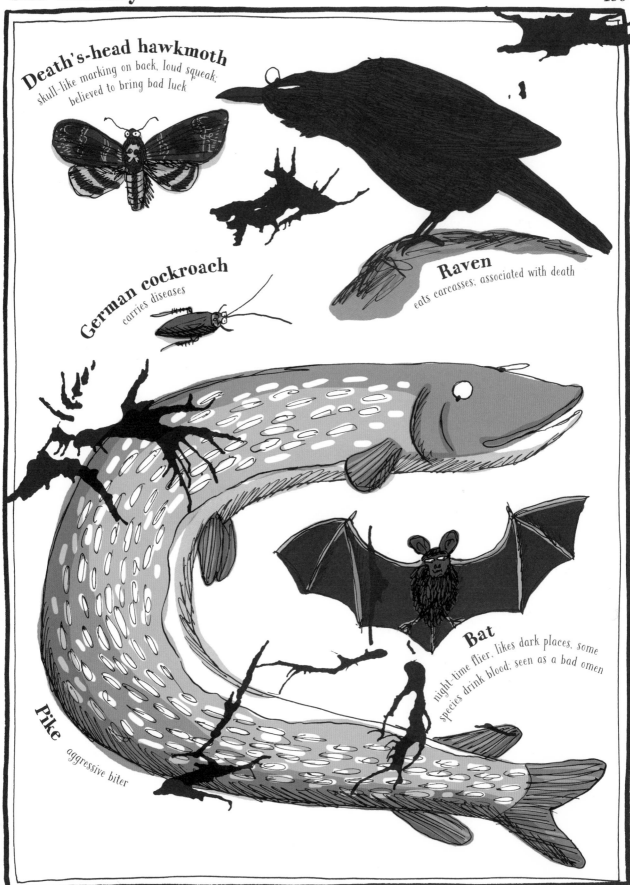

Death's-head hawkmoth
skull-like marking on back, loud squeak;
believed to bring bad luck

Raven
eats carcasses; associated with death

German cockroach
carries diseases

Bat
night-time flier, likes dark places, some
species drink blood; seen as a bad omen

Pike
aggressive biter

Great white shark attacks humans more than any other shark

Coypu carries diseases and damages crops

Wolf feared in many societies across the world

Tawny owl omen of bad luck

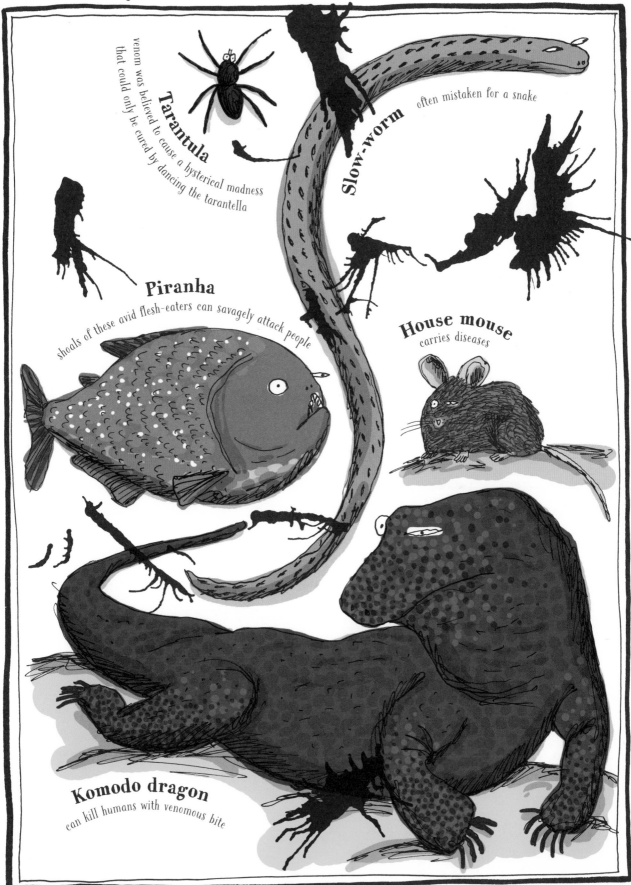

Tarantula
venom was believed to cause a hysterical madness that could only be cured by dancing the tarantella

Slow-worm often mistaken for a snake

Piranha
shoals of these avid flesh-eaters can savagely attack people

House mouse
carries diseases

Komodo dragon
can kill humans with venomous bite

Hoopoe
seen as an omen of war or death in some cultures

Fire salamander
said to be able to withstand flames

Earwig
said to pierce the eardrums of sleepers

Brown rat
carries diseases

The vanished

Dodo
† between 1662 and 1681

Steller's sea cow † 1768

Baiji † 2006

Mammoth † 12,000 years ago

Pig-footed bandicoot † 1907

Labrador duck † 1875

Rodrigues rail † 1726

Quagga † 1883

Black mamo † 1907

Great auk † 1844

Pó'ouli † 2004

Tasmanian wolf † 1936

Dinosaurs † 65 million years ago

The voyagers

Common frog
travels to lay eggs

Blue wildebeest
migrates up to 1,600 km / 1,000 mi
each year within east Africa

Emu

travels long way to reach feeding areas

Cosmopolitan butterfly

Ruff

some travel 30,000 km / 18,600 mi
each year from Siberia to Africa

Migratory locust

swarms with millions of others; can fly
more than 130 km / 80 mi per day

Arctic tern
flies up to 70,000 km / 43,000 mi each year from Arctic to Antarctic and back (longest migration of any animal)

Grey whale

Caribou
has longest land migration,
up to 6,000 km / 3,700 mi per year

Great skua
flies from Africa to northern
British Isles to breed

Leatherback sea turtle
swims up to 16,000 km / 10,000 mi each year to find jellyfish to eat

Barn swallow
flies from northern to southern hemisphere to avoid winter (at speed of 320 km / 200 mi a day)

Monarch butterfly
travels from Canada to Mexico for winter

White stork
flies up to 20,000 km / 12,400 mi a year from Europe to Africa and back

Canada goose
migrates with others in V-shape to save energy

Brown trout
swims from lakes to rivers or streams to lay eggs

European eel
travels 5,000 km / 3,100 mi to lay eggs

Acknowledgements

My heartfelt thanks:
to the jury of the City and State of Geneva's 2011 grant for book illustration,
Jean Wüest, biologist, for his valuable corrections,
Cecile Koepfli (with the help of Emily and Lucia), Mirjana and Peggy Adam Farkas,
for their help with the colouring of some families.

and also:
to my favourite sister,
my mother and my father for their constructive criticism and unconditional support,
Aldo for his advice and his comforting presence,
and to all my friends for their help and encouragement, many and varied:
Alain, Bichon, Anne HB, Aurélia, Barbara, Benjamin, Cécile, Cristina, Franky,
Ignacio, Jean-Marie, Jess, Matthew, Melanie, Mirjana, Moudja, Olga, Peggy and Valerie

—A.B.

Index

Wide Eyed Editions
www.wideeyededitions.com

Creaturepedia © Editions La Joie de Lire SA 2013

Illustrated by Adrienne Barman
Designed by Pascale Rosier

First published in Switzerland in 2013 under the title 'Drôle d'encyclopédie'
by Editions La Joie de Lire SA, 5 Chemin Neuf, CH-1207 Genève, Switzerland

First published in the English language in 2015 by
Wide Eyed Editions, an imprint of Aurum Press,
74–77 White Lion Street, London N1 9PF
www.aurumpress.co.uk

A catalogue record for this book is available from the British Library.

ISBN 978-1-84780-634-5

Illustrated digitally

Set in Didodot and Bookeyed Martin

Printed in Shenzhen, Guangdong, China

3 5 7 9 8 6 4 2